KU-707-599

Turbulent Planet

Shaky Ground

Earthquakes

Mary Colson

www.raintreepublishers.co.uk
Visit our website to find out more information about **Raintree** books.

To order:
☎ Phone 44 (0) 1865 888113
🗎 Send a fax to 44 (0) 1865 314091
🖳 Visit the Raintree Bookshop at **www.raintreepublishers.co.uk** to browse our catalogue and order online.

First published in Great Britain by Raintree Publishers,
Halley Court, Jordan Hill, Oxford
OX2 8EJ, part of Harcourt Education Ltd.
Raintree is a registered trademark of Harcourt Education Ltd.

© Harcourt Education Ltd 2005
First pu
The mo

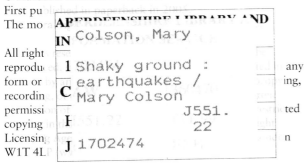
Produced for Raintree Publishers by Discovery Books Ltd.

Editorial: Charlotte Guillain, Andrew Farrow, Isabel Thomas,
Louise Galpine, and Janine de Smet
Design: Victoria Bevan and Ian Winton
Picture Research: Maria Joannou and Ginny Stroud-Lewis
Consultant: Keith Lye
Production: Jonathan Smith and Duncan Gilbert
Printed and bound in China by South China
Printing Company
Originated by Dot Gradations Ltd, UK

ISBN 1 844 43721 3 (hardback)
09 08 07 06 05
10 9 8 7 6 5 4 3 2 1

ISBN 1 844 43726 4 (paperback)
09 08 07 06 05
10 9 8 7 6 5 4 3 2 1

British Library Cataloguing in Publication Data
Colson, Mary
Shaky ground: earthquakes. – (Freestyle express. Turbulent
planet)
1. Earthquakes – Juvenile literature
I. Title
551.2'2

A full catalogue record for this book is available from the
British Library.

This levelled text is a version of Freestyle: Turbulent Planet:
Shaky Ground.

Photo acknowledgements
p.4/5, Rex Features; p.4, The Art Archive; p.5 top, Associated
Press/NOAA p.5 middle, Corbis; p.5 bottom,
Corbis/Bettmann; p.8/9, FLPA/David Hosking; p.8, Rex
Features/Sipa Press; p.10/11, Rex Features; p.11, Rex Features;
p.12, Corbis/Lloyd Cluff; p.13, Science Photo Library/David
Parker; p.14, The Regents of the University of California and
the National Information Service for Earthquake Engineering;
p.15, National Geophysical Data Center/NOAA; p.16,
NASA/Jet Propulsion Laboratory; p.17, Corbis/Bettmann; p.18
left, Corbis/Bettmann; p.18 right, Corbis; p.19, Science Photo
Library/Carlos Munoz-Yague; p.20/21, Reuters/Enny
Nurakeni; p.20, Associated Press/NOAA; p.22/23,
Corbis/Peter Turnley; p.22, Corbis Sygma/ABC Ajansi; p.23,
NASA; p.24/25, PA Photos/EPA; p.24, PA Photos/Pana-Jiji;
p.25, Popperfoto/Reuters; p.26/27, Popperfoto; p.26,
Corbis/Bettman; p.27, Corbis/Bettmann; p.28/29, Corbis; p.28,
Corbis; p.29, PA Photos/EPA; p.30 left, FLPA/USDA; p.30
right, FLPA/USDA; p.31 top, Caretas/Andes Press Agency;
p.31 bottom, Oxford Scientific Films/James H. Robinson;
p.32/33, Rex Features/Roy Garner; p.32, National Information
Service for Earthquake Engineering, University of California,
Berkeley; p.33, Rex Features/Massimo Sestini; p.34/35, PA
Photos/EPA; p.34, PA Photos/EPA; p.35, Reuters/Oswaldo
Rivas; p.36 left, Rex Features/Roy Garner; p.36 right, Corbis;
p.37, Corbis/Roger Ressmeyer; p.38/39, PA Photos/EPA; p.38,
Rex Features; p.39, The Red Cross; p.40 left, Steve
Lewis/Andes Press Agency; p.40 right, Corbis/Richard
Cummins; p.41, PA Photos/EPA; p.42/43, Getty Images News
& Sport; p.42, Lonely Planet Images; p.43, PA Photos; p.44,
Rex Features; p.45, PA Photos/Pana-Jiji

Cover photograph reproduced with permission of Corbis/
Tom Wagner

Contents

Any words appearing in the text in bold, **like this**, are explained in the glossary. You can also look out for some of them in the Wild words box at the bottom of each page.

Earthquake!

Quake history

The ancient city of Pompeii in Italy was hit by an earthquake in AD 62. It was later destroyed by a volcanic eruption in AD 79, as the picture below shows.

Imagine it is the middle of the night and you are fast asleep in bed. Suddenly you are **jolted** awake. Your heart races. The walls and floor are shaking. The bed is lifting into the air. Furniture is sliding. The glass in your window cracks and splinters. Your ears are deafened by crashes and bangs. The ground continues to shake.

Wild words   jolted   shaken suddenly

Earth-shattering

Outside, buildings crumble and roads split open. Bridges collapse and railway lines **buckle**. Gas and water pipes burst. There is no electricity and the phones are dead. Fires break out. Thick, black smoke makes it difficult to see and hard to breathe. What is happening? You are in the middle of an earthquake.

Find out later . . .

. . . what this **buoy** is used for.

. . . how the sea caused this damage.

. . . how people measure earthquakes.

△ Earthquakes can destroy even modern roads and bridges. This earthquake was in Kobe, in Japan, in 1995.

buckle   twist or bend out of shape

5

What causes earthquakes?

To understand what causes earthquakes, we need to know how the Earth is made up.

There are three main parts:
- In the middle is the ultra-hot solid inner **core** and liquid outer core.
- Around this is the mainly solid **mantle**.
- Near the top of the mantle are liquid rock and gases called **magma**.
- On the outside is the **crust**, the surface of the Earth.

Inside the Earth

The Earth is many millions of years old. The cut-away diagram below shows its different layers.

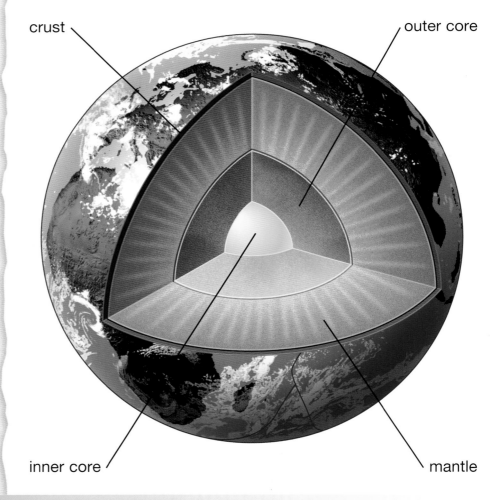

crust

outer core

inner core

mantle

Wild words continental   of one of the Earth's main land masses

Moving surface

The Earth's crust is made up of enormous **plates** or slabs. These plates are constantly moving. It is these plate movements that cause severe earthquakes. Some plates are drifting apart from each other. Others are pushing against each other.

Some plates have land on them. They are called **continental** plates. Others are under seas and oceans. They are called oceanic plates. Many plates are partly continental and partly oceanic.

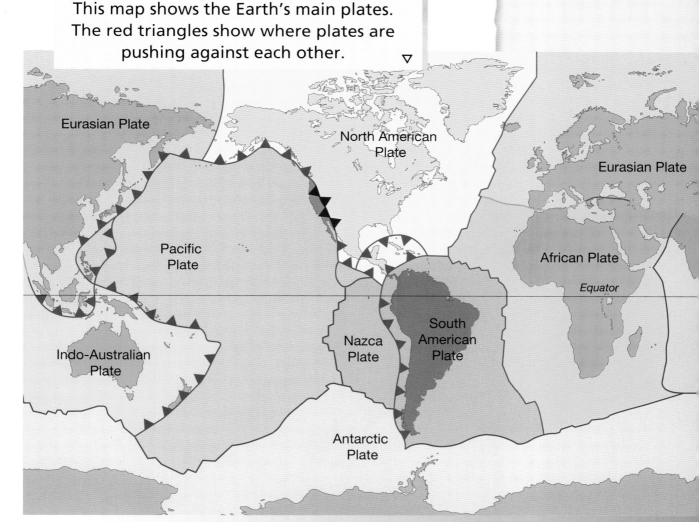

This map shows the Earth's main plates. The red triangles show where plates are pushing against each other.

Eurasian Plate

North American Plate

Eurasian Plate

Pacific Plate

African Plate

Equator

Indo-Australian Plate

Nazca Plate

South American Plate

Antarctic Plate

plate   rigid sections of the Earth's hard outer layers

Rift valleys

Rift valleys are formed when a block of the Earth's **crust** falls between two **plates** that are pulling away from each other. These valleys are usually long and deep. They have fairly flat floors and steep sides.

Rift valleys can also form under the sea on the ocean floor. This happens where two plates are separating from each other.

> The Great Rift Valley in Africa and south-west Asia is about 7200 kilometres (4500 miles) long. It has steep sides up to 2 kilometres (1 mile) high in places. ▽

Magma

Magma is **molten** rock and gas that lies beneath the Earth's crust. The magma fills any gap that opens up as two plates move apart. When it cools, new rock is formed on the surface.

Faults

A **fault** is a fracture or split in the Earth's crust. It is caused by huge **stresses** due to plate movements. Faults can measure from a few centimetres to many hundreds of kilometres long. The place where a fault happens is called a fault line.

Mid-Atlantic Ridge

On the ocean floor, the African Plate and South American plates are moving apart by about 5 centimetres (2 inches) every year. This has caused a great ridge to form.

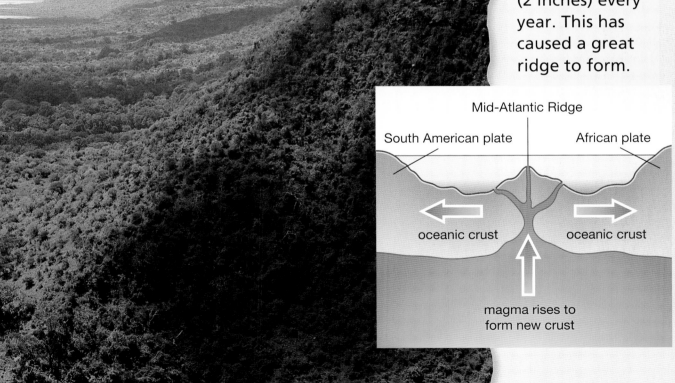

Mid-Atlantic Ridge

South American plate   African plate

oceanic crust   oceanic crust

magma rises to form new crust

stress   resistance to pressure

Fault lines

The movement along a **fault** line may happen in slow stages. It may also occur very suddenly if there is a major earthquake. Most large fault lines have taken millions of years to develop. When a fault line cracks open, the rocks may move in several directions. A road may **buckle** or a neat line of trees can become crooked.

The Mariana Trench

Down in the Pacific Ocean is the world's deepest ocean **trench**. It has been formed because the oceanic **plate** is being dragged beneath the **continental** plate, as the diagram shows.

oceanic plate

ocean trench

volcano

continental plate

magma

mantle

An earthquake twisted this ▷ railway track out of shape where it crossed a fault line.

Sudden shock

A severe earthquake happens when plate movement causes **pressure** to build up in rock layers. Rocks can absorb the strain for hundreds or even thousands of years. Eventually they crack at their weakest point. The energy is then released suddenly. This makes the ground shake. These movements are called **seismic** waves or **shockwaves**.

Gujarat quake

An earthquake hit Gujarat in India on 26 January 2001. The worst damage was in a town called Bhuj. The picture below shows families leaving Bhuj after the earthquake.

shockwave   huge burst of energy that is released from the Earth during an earthquake

Pressure points

Earthquakes also happen when two **plates** try to slide past each other. Enormous **pressure** builds up over time. The pressure may be released from time to time by tiny earthquakes.

When the plates become completely locked for a long time and then break free, a massive earthquake may occur.

A **fault** line crack in the Earth can be seen clearly at Red Canyon, Montana, in the USA. ▽

creepmeter   instrument that measures the movement along a fault line

Measuring movements

Scientists use machines called **seismometers**. The readings from seismometers help scientists measure the strength and direction of an earthquake. The readings also measure how long an earthquake lasts. For a picture of a seismometer, see page 17.

Creepmeters are underground **devices**. They measure the movement along a fault line. This tells scientists how the Earth's plates are shifting or creeping.

Creepmeter
This man has been checking an underground creepmeter. It can detect tiny ground movements which might be the first signs of a quake.

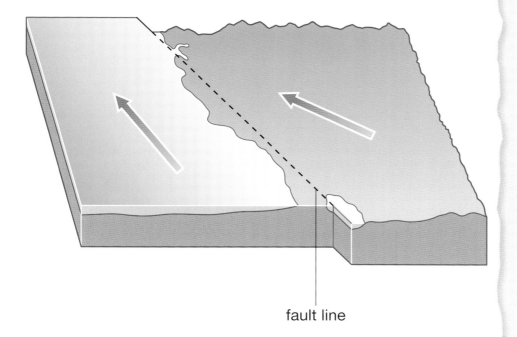

fault line

This diagram shows two plates grinding △ past each other. The huge pressure has created a fault line.

seismometer   instrument that measures the strength of shockwaves

Shake, rattle, and roll

The Pacific Ocean has more earthquakes and volcanic **eruptions** than anywhere else in the world. Many of them are too small for us to notice. The most frequent and powerful ones occur in one area. This area is called the Ring of Fire.

Quake damage

In 1994, a big earthquake struck in Northridge, Los Angeles along the San Andreas fault. The quake destroyed bridges and roads across California (above).

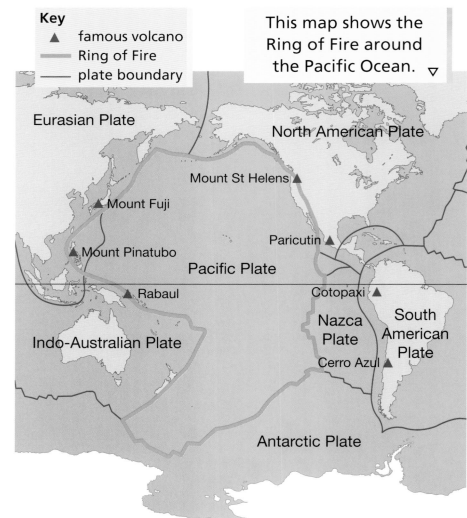

Key
- ▲ famous volcano
- ▬ Ring of Fire
- — plate boundary

This map shows the Ring of Fire around the Pacific Ocean. ▽

Eurasian Plate

North American Plate

Mount St Helens ▲

▲ Mount Fuji

Paricutin ▲

▲ Mount Pinatubo

Pacific Plate

▲ Rabaul

Cotopaxi ▲

Nazca Plate

South American Plate

Indo-Australian Plate

Cerro Azul ▲

Antarctic Plate

eruption   sudden force of gas, fire, and ash through the Earth's crust

San Andreas fault

The San Andreas **fault** stretches for more than 1000 kilometres (620 miles) along the California coast. It is close to the large cities of Los Angeles and San Francisco.

The fault lies between the Pacific plate and the North American plate. The plate movement has caused some enormous earthquakes in this region.

Quake facts

- The San Andreas fault is over 1000 kilometres (620 miles) long and about 20 kilometres (12 miles) deep

- Each week, almost 200 small quakes happen along it.

△ The San Andreas fault in California can be seen clearly in this picture.

UK quakes

Sometimes earthquakes happen in unexpected places. In 2002, two earthquakes and several **aftershocks** occurred in the UK cities of Manchester and Birmingham. Buildings shook but no damage was done. The **tremors** were felt by people up to about 130 kilometres (80 miles) away.

The UK is not near the edge of a **plate**, where most strong earthquakes take place.

Mapping movement

This image (below right) was made using **satellite** pictures before and after an earthquake. Where the coloured bands are narrower, the ground moved more violently.

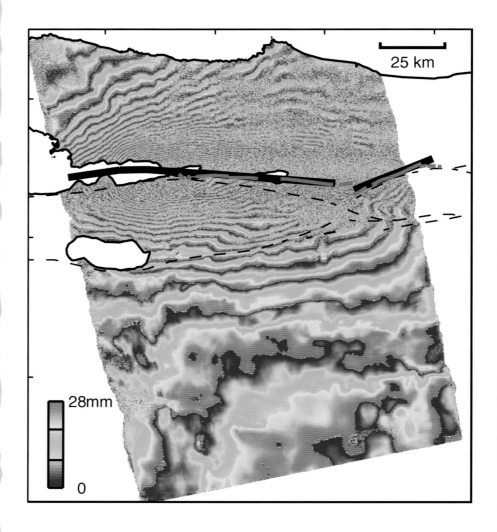

25 km

28mm

0

aftershock   delayed shaking that follows a larger earthquake

Shaken awake

Alan Odeku was fast asleep at home in Leicester, UK. He was suddenly shaken awake by a tremor. At first he did not know what was happening. Then he realised it was an earthquake. This is how he described the experience: "The shudders went on for about ten or fifteen seconds but it felt like it was much longer. The chest of drawers moved across the bedroom floor and a lamp fell off the table."

Seismometer

This machine measures **shockwaves**. Scientists, called **seismologists**, use it to help them tell how strong an earthquake was, how long it lasted, and in which direction the shockwaves were going.

SCOTLAND

Edinburgh

Leeds

Manchester

Liverpool

Leicester

WALES   Birmingham

ENGLAND

Cardiff
Bristol   London

This map shows ▷ the area of the UK where tremors were felt around Manchester in 2002.

Predicting earthquakes

There are not many warnings that an earthquake is on the way. Sometimes a series of gentle shakes, or **foreshocks,** will be the most common sign. Other clues may be bulging or swelling of the land surface.

Some people have noticed that the water level of wells changes before an earthquake. The water in ponds and canals may give off a strange smell. This is caused by the release of gases underground. The temperature of ground water becomes warmer. Animals may become jumpy, as if they know what is going to happen.

Charles Richter

In 1935, an American, Charles Richter, (below) invented the Richter scale. It measures the strength of earthquakes. The scale starts at 0. A major earthquake will measure more than 7.

Just the chimneys of some buildings were left standing after the San
▽ Francisco earthquake of 1906.

foreshock   small tremor before the main earthquake

Measuring earthquakes

The Richter scale is used for measuring the power of an earthquake. It measures how much the ground shakes from the centre of the quake.

An earthquake of less than 3.5 on the scale will hardly be noticed. One that measures between 4 and 6 will be felt by most people. The effects will vary from slight shaking in the ground to loose objects rocking. An earthquake of 6 to 7 will be quite serious. Walls crack and fall. Some houses may collapse. An earthquake that measures 8 on the scale will cause a huge amount of damage to a city.

Drawn out
A **seismogram** is a drawing of the measurement of earth **tremors**. The seismogram below shows an earthquake that measured 7.2 on the Richter scale.

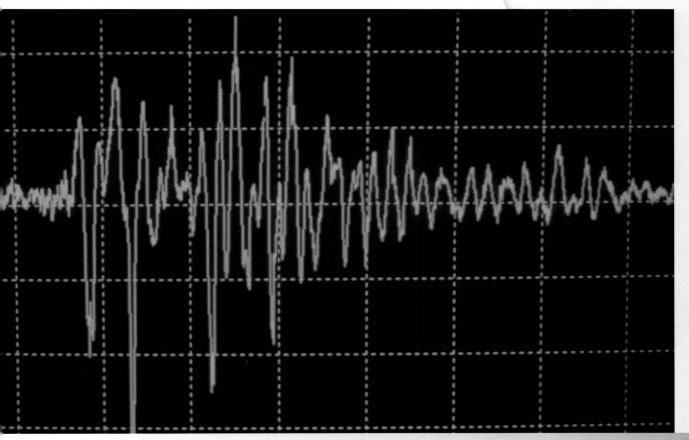

seismogram drawing of shockwave patterns

Shaken to the core

An earthquake beneath the seafloor can cause a gigantic wave called a **tsunami**. A powerful surge of water is set up underwater. It travels outwards in all directions at speeds up of to 800 kilometres (500 miles) per hour. When the tsunami reaches the shoreline it suddenly rolls up to heights of over 30 metres (100 feet). It can cause terrible destruction inland.

The city of Banda Aceh in Indonesia was wiped out by a tsunami in 2004. ▽

Measuring waves

This is a tsunami **buoy**. It is put in the sea to measure wave patterns and give early warning of a tsunami. Most tsunamis occur in the Pacific Ocean.

buoy   floating marker

Indian Ocean tsunami, 2004

On 26 December 2004, south-east Asia was hit by a terrifying tsunami. It was caused by a massive earthquake that measured 9 on the Richter scale. Huge waves raced across the ocean. The waves reached heights of up to 10 metres (33 feet). They slammed into Indonesia, Thailand, India, and Sri Lanka.

Whole towns and villages were wiped out. About 250,000 people died. Many people are still missing. The total number of deaths may never be known.

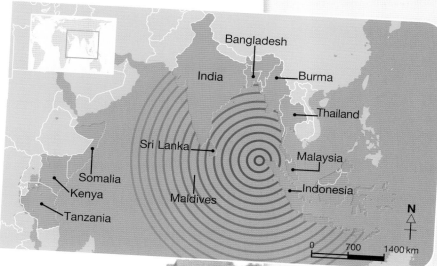

Tsunami map
The map shows the point where the earthquake happened. It shows how far the waves travelled outwards and how many countries they reached.

tsunami   huge wave caused by an earthquake beneath the ocean floor

◁ An earthquake has flattened some of these apartment blocks.

Armenian quake disaster

Armenia is a country in Europe. On 7 December 1988, a powerful earthquake shook northern Armenia. It measured 6.9 on the Richter scale. The quake was followed by a large **aftershock** of 5.8 on the scale. The earthquakes destroyed many houses, schools, factories, and office blocks. About half a million people were made homeless. The entire landscape was changed and lives were altered forever.

Flattened cities

It is hard to imagine the effects of the Armenian quake. The force was so enormous. Cracks several metres deep appeared in the rocks. Four cities and towns were flattened.

Lost contact

Communication with the outside world was lost as cables were ripped apart. Pipelines and railway tracks were destroyed. The number of dead was estimated at 25,000.

Moonquakes
An earthquake on the Moon is called a moonquake. Most moonquakes are weaker than earthquakes. This picture shows the surface of the Moon.

△ This Armenian woman lost her home in the 1988 quake.

Kobe, 1995

On 17 January 1995, a very strong earthquake shook Kobe. Kobe is a city in southern Japan. The quake measured 7.2 on the Richter scale. The ground moved for only about twenty seconds. But the effects were disastrous. More than 5000 people were killed. About 300,000 people were made homeless. More than 100,000 buildings were destroyed.

Motorway collapse

The Kobe-Osaka raised motorway was designed to wobble but not topple over in an earthquake. But when the 1995 quake hit Kobe, several sections of it collapsed (below).

Stephani's story

Stephani lived in Kobe. This is her **account** of the earthquake: 'I did not know what was happening. Was it an explosion or a bomb? I could not see. But I felt my way through. I ran out of my flat. I huddled under the **stairwell** with my neighbour. After the shaking stopped, I ran down the street. I helped people who were climbing out of the rubble.'

Hard to believe

About 300 fires raged across Kobe after gas pipes cracked. They destroyed more than 7000 wooden buildings, as shown below.

◁ Most homes in this part of Nagata, in Kobe, were flattened or burnt.

stairwell   space under a staircase

The earthquake (below) in Lisbon, Portugal in 1775 was huge. It caused waves on the surface of **Loch Ness** in Scotland, more than 2000 kilometres (1240 miles) away.

Northridge nightmare

Earthquakes in cities cause the most damage. It can cost millions to rebuild a city.

In 1994, the town of Northridge, California suffered a serious earthquake. Ten bridges collapsed and sections of eleven major roadways had to close.

The main weakness was in the design of the bridges. The concrete columns in the bridges were weak. We have now learned how to strengthen bridges to make them more quake-proof.

The broken columns ▷ on the right used to hold up a Japanese motorway.

avalanche   mass of snow and ice falling down a mountainside

Alaska, USA, 1964

An earthquake struck Alaska on Good Friday, 27 March 1964. It lasted for four minutes, causing **landslides** and **avalanches**. Buildings rocked, bridges **buckled**, and houses cracked apart. The city of Anchorage was destroyed.

Tsunami flood

Five hours after the first **tremor**, a **tsunami** crashed along the Alaskan coast. The effects were felt 5000 kilometres (3100 miles) away. It caused flooding on the coast of Hawaii.

Alaskan quake

This picture shows some of the damage caused by the 1964 quake. A whole street and a row of cars dropped 6 metres (20 feet) below normal level!

landslide   downward movement of land that can carry whole hillsides away

After-effects

Deadly mudslide

In 1970 an earthquake disturbed ice in the Andes Mountains in Peru. The ice melted and mixed with the earth to form a huge mudslide. It buried the town of Yungay (below). Many people were killed.

Even after the ground has stopped shaking, the **after-effects** of an earthquake continue. The San Francisco earthquake of 1906 is one of the worst disasters in the history of the USA. Fires burned out of control for three days. The fires destroyed 30 schools and 80 churches. More than 250,000 people were made homeless. Over 3000 people died.

This picture shows the fires in the San Francisco ▽ quake of 1906.

Wild words   after-effect   something that follows the main action

Fire frenzy: San Francisco, 1906

The 1906 San Francisco earthquake and fires destroyed almost the entire city centre. Many wooden buildings burned quickly. Firefighters were helpless against such a mighty blaze. After the quake, people worked together to rebuild the city.

Burning building

San Francisco's tallest building at the time was the Call skyscraper (above). It survived the quake but burned down in the fires that followed.

Factfile
St Helens

- Ten million trees were flattened

- Almost 300 kilometres (185 miles) of roads were destroyed

- 57 people and thousands of animals were killed.

Mount St Helens

When an earthquake rocks a volcano, things really get dangerous. That is what happened in 1980 to Mount St Helens. Mount St Helens is a volcano in the north-west of the USA. The quake struck about 1.5 kilometres (0.9 miles) beneath the volcano.

The earthquake started a gigantic **landslide** followed by an **avalanche**.

The eruption blasted a huge crater in the top of the volcano. ▽

Beautiful Mount St Helens before the eruption. ▽

After-effects

Within two weeks, the ash from the eruption had travelled around the world. **Geologists** were shocked at the speed and power of the eruption. Even now the landscape has not returned to its former beauty.

Etna erupts

Mount Etna on the Italian island of Sicily is the highest volcano in Europe. In 2002 an earthquake, which measured 4.4 on the Richter scale, caused this spectacular eruption.

△ Ten years after the eruption, the land around Mount St Helens was still covered in ash and dead trees.

geologist   scientist who studies rocks

Bedrock

Bedrock is the layer of rock that lies beneath the soil and loose rock on the surface. Houses built directly on the bedrock are less likely to be damaged by earth **tremors**. It is better to build on solid rock like granite. Houses built on soft surfaces like clay and sand are less resistant to **shockwaves**.

Quake facts

In 1959 a big earthquake hit Montana, USA. As the picture below shows, a motorway slumped into a lake. Twenty-eight people died.

bedrock layer of rock that lies beneath soil and loose rock

Sinking soil

Soft soils can be a big problem in an earthquake. The heat and **pressure** from the quake can make the ground so hot or crumbly that it is almost liquid. This is called **liquefaction**. Houses built on liquefied ground will sink into it. Soft soils on hillsides can turn into mudslides, taking whole houses down with them.

Assisi

The Italian town of Assisi was hit by earthquakes in 1997. Part of the roof of the church of St Francis fell in (below).

◁ The hard concrete just below this road surface has cracked and moved in all directions.

Search and rescue

After an earthquake it is a race against time to find survivors. Rescue teams use **infra-red cameras**. They can detect the heat of a human body. **Sniffer dogs** help to find people trapped beneath fallen buildings.

Reaching the disaster

Sometimes it is hard for ambulances and rescue teams to reach the disaster area. Roads may have collapsed or been blocked during the earthquake.

Bingol, 2003

A school **dormitory** in the town of Bingol collapsed when an earthquake shook Turkey in 2003. Almost 200 sleeping students were trapped inside. In the picture below, a sniffer dog hunts for survivors.

Italian search and rescue teams looking for survivors at San Giuliano di Puglia. ▷

San Giuliano di Puglia

In 2002, an earthquake struck San Giuliano di Puglia. This is a small village in southern Italy. Many buildings collapsed. A school roof fell in, burying children alive. Rescue workers pulled at least 34 people, mostly children, from the rubble.

Airlift

Rescue workers are trained to work with helicopters. In this picture, a worker is being lowered in a stretcher, which will lift an injured person.

infra-red camera camera that detects heat to show up human bodies

Surviving an earthquake

What people should do if an earthquake strikes …

During a quake:

1. Stay calm
2. **If you are inside:** climb under a table or desk. Cover yourself with anything within reach, and hold on
3. Stay away from windows and glass dividers
4. **If you are outside:** stand away from buildings, trees, and telephone and electric power lines
5. Stay still until the shaking stops.

Drop, cover, and hold on

Remember the simple motto: drop, cover, and hold on. This means drop to the floor, lie under a table to avoid being hit by falling objects, and wait until the shaking is over.

△ This woman is lying in an earthquake-proof bed with a strong roof to shelter her.

After a quake:

1. Check for injuries
2. Provide first aid
3. Check for safety: turn off gas, water, and electricity
4. Put on long trousers, a long-sleeved top, sturdy shoes, and gloves
5. Turn on the radio and listen for safety instructions
6. Expect **aftershocks**. Each time you feel one: drop, cover, and hold on.

Packed for survival

Lots of companies in the USA give their workers earthquake survival packs. These contain useful survival objects like a torch, matches, a cloth mask, and even playing cards!

Items in a typical earthquake survival pack. ▽

Facing disaster

Many people who live in earthquake zones need to prepare for **tremors**. They store food, bottled water, torches, a radio, and a first aid kit. Every year on 1 September, there is a Disaster Prevention Day **drill** in Japan. Millions of people practise what they should do if there is an earthquake.

These children in Kagoshima, Japan, are wearing protective hats. ▽

To the rescue

In the picture above, Leyla, a 3-year-old girl, is rescued from her school **dormitory**. She was trapped there by the Bingol earthquake in Turkey in May 2003.

drill   practice

Worldwide help

When a major earthquake strikes, countries around the world offer help. The United Nations, the Red Cross, and the World Food Programme are also quick to respond. They send doctors, **engineers**, helicopters, and rescue equipment. They also supply blankets, medicines, and tents.

Leaflets about earthquake survival can be found on the Internet. ▷

Earthquake

USGS

American Red Cross

Are You Ready for an Earthquake?
Here's what you can do to prepare for such an emergency

Prepare a Home Earthquake Plan

✔ Choose a safe place in every room—under a sturdy table or desk or against an inside wall where nothing can fall on you.

✔ Practice DROP, COVER, AND HOLD ON at least twice a year. Drop under a sturdy desk or table, hold on, and protect your eyes by pressing your face against your arm. If there's no table or desk nearby, sit on the floor against an interior wall away from windows, bookcases, or tall furniture that could fall on you. Teach children to DROP, COVER, AND HOLD ON!

✔ Choose an out-of-town family contact.

✔ Consult a professional to find out additional ways you can protect your home, such as bolting the house to its foundation and other structural mitigation techniques.

✔ Take a first aid class from your local Red Cross chapter. Keep your training current.

✔ Get training in how to use a fire extinguisher from your local fire department.

✔ Inform babysitters and caregivers of your plan.

Eliminate hazards, by—

✔ Bolting bookcases, china cabinets, and other tall furniture to wall studs.

✔ Installing strong latches on cupboards.

✔ Strapping the water heater to wall studs.

Prepare a Disaster Supplies Kit for home and car, including—

✔ First aid kit and essential medications.

✔ Canned food and can opener.

✔ At least three gallons of water per person.

✔ Protective clothing, rainwear, and bedding or sleeping bags.

✔ Battery-powered radio, flashlight, and extra batteries.

✔ Special items for infant, elderly, or disabled family members.

✔ Written instructions for how to turn off gas, electricity, and water if authorities advise you to do so. (Remember, you'll need a professional to turn natural gas service back on.)

✔ Keeping essentials, such as a flashlight and sturdy shoes, by your bedside.

Know what to do when the shaking begins

✔ DROP, COVER, AND HOLD ON! Move only a few steps to a nearby safe place. Stay indoors until the shaking stops and you're sure it's safe to exit. Stay away from windows. In a high-rise building, expect the fire alarms and sprinklers to go off during a quake.

✔ If you are in bed, hold on and stay there, protecting your head with a pillow.

✔ If you are outdoors, find a clear spot away from buildings, trees, and power lines. Drop to the ground.

✔ If you are in a car, slow down and drive to a clear place (as described above). Stay in the car until the shaking stops.

Identify what to do after the shaking stops

✔ Check yourself for injuries. Protect yourself from further danger by putting on long pants, a long-sleeved shirt, sturdy shoes, and work gloves.

✔ Check others for injuries. Give first aid for serious injuries.

✔ Look for and extinguish small fires. Eliminate fire hazards. Turn off the gas if you smell gas or think it's leaking. (Remember, only a professional should turn it back on.)

✔ Listen to the radio for instructions.

✔ Expect aftershocks. Each time you feel one, DROP, COVER, AND HOLD ON!

✔ Inspect your home for damage. Get everyone out if your home is unsafe.

✔ Use the telephone only to report life-threatening emergencies.

Your local contact is:

engineer   person who designs and builds things like machines, roads, and bridges

The future

Still standing

Bamboo and wood are strong and flexible. These bamboo and wood homes are in the Andes Mountains of South America. They stay standing even after massive earthquakes.

We do not know how to prevent earthquakes. But we can make sure they cause as little damage as possible. For example, **engineers** are finding new ways to make buildings safer, stronger, and more flexible. Some **high-rises** are being built on rollers or tough rubber springs. This allows them to sway when the ground shakes.

The 260-metre (853-feet) high Transamerica Pyramid in San Francisco (left) has been designed to withstand strong earthquakes.

Thinking ahead

California is probably better prepared for earthquakes than anywhere else in the world. There are strict building laws. All new buildings are designed to cope with quakes. It is against the law to build on or across a **fault** line. San Francisco, for example, has wide streets which help to prevent the spread of fire. The extra width also allows buildings to sway without crashing into each other.

Pagoda design

Japanese buildings called **pagodas** swing and sway but almost never give way in an earthquake. We can learn much from the design of wooden towers like this one in Japan.

pagoda   Hindu or Buddhist temple with a tower of several levels

Warning signs

Seismologists study **plate** movements to help them understand where earthquakes may strike. They can measure even the tiniest movements in the Earth's plates. Changes in the size of **shockwaves** and swellings in the ground are just some of the warning signs that a quake is building up.

Dramatic Djibouti

It is hard to believe from the peaceful-looking picture of Djibouti, in Africa (above), that it suffers from frequent earth **tremors**. Djibouti lies at the edges of two plates that are moving apart.

In countries like the USA, buildings can be strengthened against future earthquakes. Here, an **engineer** is checking protection ▽ underneath City Hall, Los Angeles, USA.

Turbulent planet

Each year, about 500,000 tremors occur within the Earth's **crust**. Most of them go unnoticed. About 1000 earthquakes cause some damage. But sometimes there is a major earthquake that brings disaster. Scientists hope that they can predict earthquakes better. Fewer lives may be lost in the future.

Emergency services

Some countries have Disaster Plans. These explain to the public what the police, army, firefighters, and hospitals will do if an earthquake hits.

△ Huge traffic problems are created by earthquake damage to roads.

Find out more

Websites

Earthquakes

British Geological Survey
Full of information on UK earthquakes and more.
www.quakes.bgs.ac.uk

Worldwide Earthquake Locator

Maps and information about quakes around the world. Updated daily.
www.geo.ed.ac.uk/quakexe/quakes

BBC Science

News, features, and activities on natural disasters.
www.bbc.co.uk/science

Books

Disasters in Nature: Earthquakes,
   Patience Coster (Heinemann Library, 2000)
Nature on the Rampage: Earthquakes,
   Tami Deedrick (Raintree, 2003)
Nature on the Rampage: Tsunamis,
   Christy Steele (Raintree, 2003)

World Wide Web

To find out more about earthquakes you can search the Internet. Use keywords like these:

- earthquake +[country]
- seismologist
- "sniffer dog" +earthquake

You can find your own keywords by using words from this book. The search tips opposite will help you find useful websites.

Search tips

There are billions of pages on the Internet. It can be difficult to find exactly what you are looking for. These tips will help you find useful websites more quickly:

- Know what you want to find out
- Use simple keywords
- Use two to six keywords in a search
- Only use names of people, places, or things
- Put double quote marks around words that go together, for example "plate movement"

Where to look

Search engine

A search engine looks through millions of website pages. It lists all the sites that match the words in the search box. You will find the best matches are at the top of the list, on the first page.

Search directory

A person instead of a computer has sorted a search directory. You can search by keyword or subject and browse through the different sites. It is like looking through books on a library shelf.

Glossary

account   story of what happened

after-effect   something that follows the main action

aftershock   delayed shaking that follows a larger earthquake

avalanche   mass of snow and ice falling down a mountainside

bedrock   layer of rock that lies beneath soil and loose rock

buckle   twist or bend out of shape

buoy   floating marker

continental   of one of the Earth's main land masses

core   ultra-hot centre of the Earth

creepmeter   instrument that measures the movement along a fault line

crust   outer, solid surface of the Earth

device   machine or instrument

dormitory   sleeping room with several beds

drill   practice

engineer   person who designs and builds things like machines, roads, and bridges

eruption   sudden force of gas, fire, and ash through the Earth's crust

fault   fracture or split in the Earth's crust

foreshock   small tremor before the main earthquake

geologist   scientist who studies rocks

high-rise   building with many floors

infra-red camera   camera that detects heat to show up human bodies

jolted   shaken suddenly

landslide   downward movement of land that can carry whole hillsides away

liquefaction   process of becoming liquid

loch   Scottish word for lake

magma   very hot mixture of liquid rock and gases

mantle   Earth's layer that lies between the core and the crust

molten   melted

pagoda   Hindu or Buddhist temple with a tower of several levels

plate   rigid sections of the Earth's hard, outer layers

pressure   pushing force

rift valley   long, deep valley with flat floor and steep sides

satellite   device orbiting the Earth that has been sent up into space by a rocket

seismic   to do with earthquakes

seismogram   drawing of shockwave patterns

seismologist   scientist who studies earthquakes

seismometer   instrument that measures the strength of shockwaves

shockwave   huge burst of energy that is released from the Earth during an earthquake

sniffer dogs   dogs trained to find survivors
by smell

stairwell   space under a staircase

stress   resistance to pressure

tremor   movement in the ground caused
by an earthquake

trench   long, deep ditch or groove

tsunami   huge wave caused by an
earthquake beneath the ocean floor

Index

Titles in the *Freestyle Express: Turbulent Planet* series include:

Hardback   1 844 43704 3

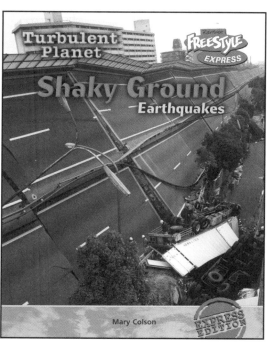

Hardback   1 844 43721 3

Hardback   1 844 43722 1

Hardback   1 844 43723 X

Find out about other Freestyle Express titles on our website www.raintreepublishers.co.uk